W9-CGT-024

ORANGE JUICE

by Gretchen Will Mayo

Reading consultant: Susan Nations, M.Ed., author/literacy coach/consultant

J663.63
MAY

Please visit our web site at: www.earlyliteracy.cc
For a free color catalog describing Weekly Reader® Early Learning Library's
list of high-quality books, call 1-877-445-5824 (USA) or 1-800-387-3178 (Canada).
Weekly Reader® Early Learning Library's fax: (414) 336-0164.

Library of Congress Cataloging-in-Publication Data available upon request from publisher.
Fax (414) 336-0157 for the attention of the Publishing Records Department.

ISBN 0-8368-4068-2 (lib. bdg.)
ISBN 0-8368-4075-5 (softcover)

This edition first published in 2004 by
Weekly Reader® Early Learning Library
330 West Olive Street, Suite 100
Milwaukee, WI 53212 USA

Copyright © 2004 by Weekly Reader® Early Learning Library

Editor: JoAnn Early Macken
Art direction, cover and layout design: Tammy Gruenewald
Photo research: Diane Laska-Swanke

Photo credits: Cover, title, pp. 4, 5, 6, 8, 9, 11, 12, 13, 14, 15, 17, 18, 19, 20 © Gregg Andersen;
pp. 7, 16 © Tammy Gruenewald; p. 10 © Gibson Stock Photography

All rights reserved. No part of this book may be reproduced, stored in a retrieval system,
or transmitted in any form or by any means, electronic, mechanical, photocopying, recording,
or otherwise, without the prior written permission of the copyright holder.

Printed in the United States of America

1 2 3 4 5 6 7 8 9 08 07 06 05 04

Table of Contents

An orange is a good snack.

Orange Juice Time

People in many places love oranges. They are loaded with vitamins. They help kids grow strong and stay healthy. Orange juice is good for you, too. Is orange juice just for breakfast? No way!

You can get vitamin C from orange juice.
Vitamin C helps keep you from catching colds.
Orange juice also gives bodies important minerals.
Minerals help build bone and muscles. Orange
juice is a healthy choice for kids.

Which one is the healthy choice?

In groves, oranges grow on long rows of trees.

Growing Oranges

In the United States, oranges are the third most popular fruit. Only bananas and apples are eaten more often. Florida, California, and Arizona have large orange groves. Many people in warm places grow orange trees in their yards.

Cold weather is hard on orange trees. Cold can damage orange skins. Freezing can ruin the fruit. Most orange juice comes from two very warm places. It comes from Florida in North America. It comes from Brazil in South America.

Oranges grow in warm places.

FLORIDA

BRAZIL

Juicy Valencias are only one of
many kinds of oranges.

Oranges are different sizes and flavors. Some
have no seeds. Some have thicker skins. Some
are juicier or sweeter than others. Each type of
orange has its own growing season. Most North
American oranges grow from October until April.

Oranges are berries that grow on trees. Some fruit grows riper after it is picked. Peaches and pears do. Oranges do not. They must ripen on the tree.

Oranges grow on an orange tree.

A worker picks oranges in Florida.

Orange growers sample the fruit. They test it to
see if it is ripe. In Florida, most oranges are
picked by hand.

Workers dump the oranges into plastic tubs.
Each tub holds about 900 pounds (400 kilograms).
A special truck called a "goat" picks up the tubs.

A tub of oranges is carried to a processing plant.

Oranges are weighed on a scale.

The goat dumps the load into a tractor-trailer. The trailer carries the oranges to a processing plant. The oranges are weighed. The grower is paid for each pound of oranges.

At the plant, the oranges are washed. Workers take out the damaged fruit. Then the oranges are sorted by size.

A worker takes away damaged oranges.

The extractor squeezes out juice and leaves the other parts of the orange.

Squeezing and Packaging

A machine called an extractor squeezes juice from the oranges. It pricks the skins to remove orange oils. These oils can be made into cleaning products. Then the extractor squeezes out the juice. Pulp, seeds, and peels are strained out. They can be made into cattle feed.

Some juice may be pasteurized at once.
Pasteurizing means heating the juice to kill germs
and mold. This juice is packaged and sold. It is
ready to drink.

A machine pasteurizes the orange juice.

Concentrated orange juice comes in cans.

Some juice is sent to a machine that takes most of the water out. The juice that remains is called concentrate. A refrigerated tanker carries it to a packaging plant. There it is packaged and frozen. Then the concentrate can be shipped safely. It may travel to other states or other countries.

Some of the concentrate is mixed with water.
Adding water makes the juice ready to drink.

A machine mixes orange juice and water.

Juice made from concentrate is
called reconstituted.

Some orange juice sold in stores is made from
concentrate.

Many dairy plants also package orange juice. The same machines pasteurize and package orange juice and milk. Before juice is sent through the machines, all of the milk is cleaned away.

A dairy worker cleans a machine.

Orange juice makes a tasty
after-school drink.

Orange Juice in Any Form

Have your orange juice any way you like. You
can squeeze your own fresh oranges. You can
buy juice that is ready to drink. You can mix
water with frozen concentrate.

Try all the styles of orange juice. Each one is delicious!

Fruit and juice are part of the food pyramid.

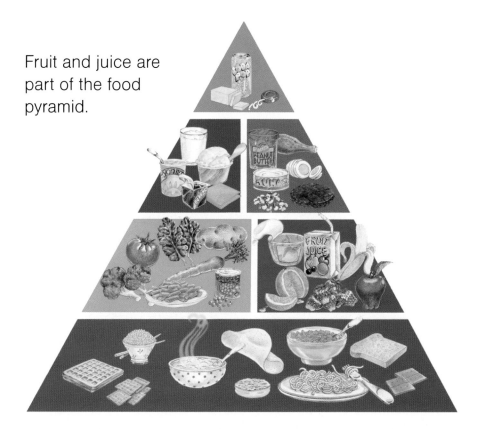

Glossary

extractor — a machine that takes out a certain substance

groves — areas of land where trees are planted

mold — a fungus that forms a fuzzy coating on damp surfaces

pricks — pierces with a pointed object

pulp — the soft, juicy part of fruit

refrigerated — kept cool or cold

ripe — fully grown and developed

strained — pressed or poured through a filter to separate liquids from solids

For More Information

Books

Arnosky, Jim. *Armadillo's Orange*. NY: G. P. Putnam's Sons, 2003.

Chessen, Betsey and Chanko, Pamela. *Orange Juice*. NY: Scholastic, 1998.

Snyder, Inez. *Oranges to Orange Juice*. *How Things Are Made* Series. NY: Children's Press, 2003.

Spilsbury, Louise. *Oranges*. *Food* Series. Chicago: Heinemann Library, 2002.

Web Sites

The Best Ways to Start Your Day

www.floridajuice.com/floridacitrus/weekly_reader/students_home.html
Reading adventure, activities, and Florida OJ road tour

The Story of Florida Orange Juice

members.aol.com/citrusweb/oj_story.html
How oranges are harvested and processed

Fresh for Kids

www.fandvforme.com.au/
Fruit and vegetable information and games

Index

About the Author

Gretchen Will Mayo likes to be creative with her favorite foods. In her kitchen, broccoli and corn are mixed with oranges to make a salad. She sprinkles granola on applesauce. She blends yogurt with orange juice and bananas. She experiments with different pasta sauces. When she isn't eating, Ms. Mayo writes stories and books for young people like you. She is also a teacher and illustrator. She lives in Wisconsin with her husband, Tom, who makes delicious soups. They have three adult daughters.